Guide to Plants

along the

Manukā Nature Trail

on the

Big Island of Hawai'i

Judy Hall Jacobson

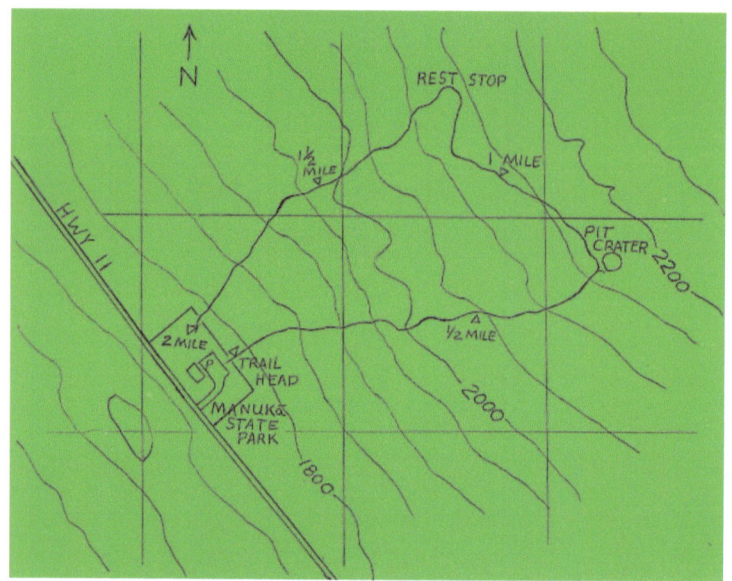

Manukā Nature Trail map drawn by Terry Jacobson

All parts of this book may be used for educational purposes. Contact the author for permission:

Windy Ridge Publishing: P.O. Box 1158, Haines, AK 99827 or judyinhaines@aptalaska.net

© 2013 by Judy Hall Jacobson

Cover photos from top and clockwise: Ohi'a, Huehue, 'Ie'ie, Kopiko and Blue Morning Glory

Manukā Nature Trail

Trail Length: 2 mile loop/ **Activity**: Pedestrian/ **Difficulty**: Moderate, wear sturdy shoes/ **Terrain**: Forested/ **Elevation Gain**: 400 ft./ **Bring**: Water, mosquito repellent, binoculars

Welcome to the **Manukā Nature Trail** which loops through part of the **Manukā Natural Area Reserve**. The **Manukā Natural Area Reserve** established in 1983, covers 24,550 acres. At the trail head, you stand on the leeward flank of Mauna Loa, the largest of all currently active volcanoes in the world. It takes up half the space of the island of Hawai'i, measuring 60 miles long and 30 miles wide. If measured from its base on the ocean floor, then its entire height is 30,080 ft. It's actual elevation is 13, 681 feet (4,170 meters) and it last erupted in 1984.

To protect the State's best remaining intact native ecosystems, Hawaii's Natural Area Reserve System, established in 1970, totals 109,000 acres. The State's Natural Area Reserve System aims to preserve Hawaii's native plants, animals and the systems and processes that maintain them. The Manukā NAR is the largest of the State's 19 natural area reserves.

"Manukā" means 'blundering' in the Hawaiian language. It was the name of an ancient land division (ahupa'a) that ran from Manukā Bay on the southwest side of the Island up the slopes of Mauna Loa.

This trail takes hikers through a forest of native, introduced and invasive Hawaiian plants and animals. Along the 2-3 hour trail, you will experience Hawaiian natural history as the trail meanders over lava flows of differing ages, through ancient Hawaiian cultural sites and past a pit crater. Be sure to take the short detour for a spectacular view of the crater. Pit craters are circular-shaped craters formed by the sinking or collapse of the ground and are common along rift zones of shield volcanoes. Since pit craters are relatively inaccessible, they harbor interesting plants and animals. Look for Papala (*Charpentiera ovata*) in the pit crater. There are several dangerous undercut areas around the pit. Be sure to view the pit inhabitants with binoculars so you do not get too close to the edge. Concentrations of the Hawaiian hoary bat have been documented in Manukā. Also near the pit is a great place to listen to and look for several of our native birds including apapane, elepaio and amakihi. Bird watching is another reason to carry binoculars. The pit crater is at the top of the loop, after which you will begin descending back toward the Manukā picnic area.

Plant information in this pamphlet is arranged so it can be followed as you hike the trail. The numbers of the plants match those of the signs. Two endemic endangered plants found in **Manukā Natural Area Reserve** but are not along the trail are Mehamehame *(Flueggea neowawraea)* and Oʻahu Chewstick *(Gouania vitifolia)*. They are included in this book.

Species in the second section do not have signs and are arranged by subsections: Trees and Shrubs, Herbs (herbaceous) and Others (ferns, vines and fungi).

Photos are by the author unless otherwise noted in the plant description. Thanks to Kim and Forest Starr and David Eickhoff for permission to include their excellent photos here. A huge thanks also goes to Terry Jacobson for photos and hiking the Nature Trail many, many times to do research for this book.

Some definitions: An endemic species is found in a given region or location (in Hawaii sometimes only on one island or only along the Hawaiian Chain) and nowhere else in the world. A plant is indigenous if it came to a region without the help of humans. It is introduced if it arrived with the help of humans. A naturalized plant came with the help of humans and reproduces in its new environment spreading to natural areas. Invasive species are introduced where they did not evolve and have no natural enemies to reduce their spread. A weed is any plant species, native or exotic, whose presence is undesirable to people in a particular time or place.

Check out the 8-acre arboretum in the **Manukā Wayside Park**. From 1930-1950, over 130 introduced exotic species were planted here along with 48 species of native Hawaiian plants and trees. Many of them have succumbed to drought and disease over the years. There are plans to label and replant trees and other plants in the wayside park.

Please enjoy this nature hike and remember it is your kuleana (responsibility) to maintain pono (respect) for the aina (land) and all that comes from the aina. Mahalo.

Table of Contents

Plants with signs:

end=endemic, ind=indigenous, pol=Polynesian introduction
intro=introduced nat=naturalized inva=invasive   Page

Species included without signs (in book order):

Trees and Shrubs:

Herbs:

All Others

Unfortunately, since this book was published, many new introduced and invasive species have taken over along the trail and so as yet, are not included.

Plants with Signs:
1. Metrosideros polymorpha -- Ohi'a
Endemic/Myrtaceae/Myrtle Family

Ohi'a is the most common native tree in Hawaii and along the **Manukā Nature Trail**. The species name means (poly) many and (morpha) forms. It varies in appearance and grows in many habitats, and is also often the first tree to grow on new lava. Ohi'a is a prostrate shrub in dry areas and in mid to upper dry to cloud forests, and a tree up to 100 ft. tall. The bark is rough, fissured, light gray to sometimes black; in moist areas covered with mistletoe, ferns, herbs, mosses, lichens and liverworts. Leaves opposite, alternate, small, ½ to 2 inches long, varying in shape and texture. Flowers have inconspicuous petals with long red stamens. The nectar-rich flowers are important as a food source for several endemic bird species including 'apapane. It is considered sacred to Pele the goddess of fire.

Legend has it, if you pick a lehua flower on the way up a mountain, you will cause the weather to cloud over in a thick mist or rain. It is allowed to pick flowers on the way out of the forest. The dark, hard wood used to make the mo'o (gunwale) on canoes and for posts in house construction. This beautiful and durable wood used for poi boards, bowls, ukulele fret boards, spoons and temple carvings. Young reddish-green to crimson leaves called liko lehua, are steeped to make a tonic tea. This genus has been reclassified in Hawai'i and there are now 5 endemic species recognized. Leaves may be affected by the Puccinia rust which starts as yellow powdery spots or as circular patterns on the leaf and shoot. A new fungal disease known as Rapid Ohi'a Death, is currently attacking and killing Ohi'a. One species also considered a variety, *M. macropus* almost always has yellow flowers. Red-flowered ohi'a photo by Terry Jacobson.

7

2. *Osteomeles anthyllidifolia* -- 'Ulei
Indigenous/Rosaceae/Hawaiian Hawthorne

A common, sprawling, vine-like shrub found in dry areas from the coast to high elevation, with small, stiff, shiny, pinnately compound leaves with smooth edges, opposite with one odd one at tip: similar in arrangement to leaves in members of the pea family. Flowers are small and white, 5-petaled, resembling a wild rose. Fruit white when ripe, rose-hip-like clusters that are edible.

Wood is hard and used for spears and o'o: a digging tool used in agriculture. Flexible young branches used in fishing nets and baskets. Berries used to make a lavender dye. Flowers popular lei-making material in old Hawai'i.

3. *Cordyline fruticosa* -- Ki
Polynesian/Liliaceae / Ti Plant

A shrub or small tree to 10 ft. growing from a thick rootstock with long, spindly stem and whorl of long, oval leaves on top. It flowers occasionally with sprays of pinkish-white, 6-petaled flowers at center of leaves. Green-leafed forms rarely produce fruit; reddish-leafed ones produce red berries.

Plant used to ward off evil spirits. Used for wrapping food (lu'au, also name of traditional Hawaiian feast), line imu for cooking and second only to pili grass as roof thatch. Medicinally used for asthma, TB, sinus congestion and more. Twisted stems used for lei or rope, or coiled to make sandals. Roots used to produce okolehau, a weak liquor. Related to hala pepe (*Peleomele* spp.) and agave. Formally included in the *Malvaceae* or mallow family.

4. *Diospyros sandwicensis* -- Lama
Endemic/ Ebenaceae /Hawaiian Persimmon

A common shrub or tree to 32 feet tall in low dry to high wet forests, often growing with Ohi'a. Bark dark gray to brown to black, rough to the touch. Leaves alternate, on opposite sides of the stem, drab gray-green pointed ovals often densely arranged on stem. Young leaves with red to pinkish tinge. Fruit yellow to orange when ripe and sweet though a bit insipid.

Tree commonly infested with a mite that produces clusters of mistletoe-like, finely branched growths 2" or so in diameter on twigs and branches. It is used to fence in sacred areas (Palama). A piece of lama wood, wrapped in yellow kapa scented with 'olena

(*Curcuma domestica* or turmeric) was placed on the alter representing the hula goddess Laka. Also used for heiau (temple) construction. Pulverized fruit used to treat skin ulcers. The sapwood is white and used for religious purposes. Lama means light or enlightenment in Hawaiian. Related to ebony.

5. *Psydrax odorata* -- Alahe'e
Indigenous/Rubiaceae/ Wild Coffee

A tree to 20 ft. tall, with smooth, white bark and horizontal branches common in dry and mesic (zone with moderate rainfall ~60 inches per year) forests. Glossy, dark green, pointed, opposite, oval leaves, 2-3 inches long. Leaves remain vibrant and shiny even in periods of drought.
It has small, fragrant, white flowers and black fleshy fruit.

When in bloom, the clusters of fragrant, bright white flowers *en mass* light up the tree. Its fragrance can be mild to very strong. The hard wood used for 'o'o (digging sticks), weapons, fish spears, adze blades and hooks. Leaves produce a black dye. It is also known as *Canthium odoratum*. The species name refers to the fragrance of the flowers. This is a common species all along the **Manukā Nature Trail**.

6. *Pipturus albidus* -- Mamaki
Endemic/Urticaceae/Hawaiian Nettle

 Shrub or small tree to 20 ft. found in mesic and wet forests up to 4,000 ft. in elevation. The leaves are 1 to 5 inches long, 1-3 inches wide, alternate, broadly oval, course with small teeth on edge and three prominent veins. Below, leaves appear almost white with fine hairs. Inconspicuous flowers along stem and whitish, dry fleshy fruit.

Favorite food of the Kamehameha butterfly (*Vanessa tame-amea*). It is used medicinally as a tea for stomach, bladder and bowel troubles. It is in the same family as Olona (*Touchardia latifolia*), the inner bark used to make rope that is 8 times stronger than hemp and in wide use around the world until nylon and synthetic rope was developed. As with many species that evolved without browsing animals, it is thornless.

7. *Aleurites moluccana* -- Kukui
Polynesian/Euphorbiaceae/Candlenut

A common, large, spreading tree reaching 70 ft. tall, found in gulches from sea level to 2,000 ft. elevation. It has grayish-white bark with flattened furrows and pale green maple-leaf like leaves. The leaves are variable and hairy on the lower surface when young. Flowers are small, white and in clusters. Large, rounded, hard-shelled nut about 1" in diameter grows inside a leathery walnut-like husk. When husks decay after falling to the ground, they leave a hard-shelled nut about an inch in diameter.

From a distance it can be told from other trees by its light grayish color. Oil from the nut was extracted and burned in lamps with a wick made of kapa. Raw nut is a laxative. Kukui was seen as a pig demigod by Hawaiians. If you take a leaf, fold it in half with crease running from tip to stem, you see the profile of a pig.

In the year of Hawaiian statehood, 1959, the legislature adopted the kukui as the state's official tree because of the many uses employed by ancient Hawaiians. The bark and juice of the nut used as a dye. The flowers, nuts and bark are medicinal. Nuts were strung together and used as a light source. Only royalty (ali'i) were allowed to wear the polished nuts. We chuckle too when we encounter this unique kukui face along the **Manukā Nature Trail**.

8. *Nestegis sandwicensis* -- Olopua
Endemic/Oleaceae/Hawaiian Olive

Shrub or tree to 35 ft. with furrowed dark gray bark, found in dry to mesic forests from 100 to 4,000 feet. The crinkly leathery leaves are 3 to 10 inches long, very dark green, opposite and lance-shaped. The upper surface of the leaves are glossy with pale yellow midribs and the lower surface even paler, often the distinctive identifying feature when it is not blooming or bearing fruit. It rarely flowers. When it does it produces seven to eleven small pale yellow, yellow-green or white flowers, clustered at the base of leaves.

The flowers have been given the Hawaiian name nonohina. The fruits are oval and start out green and mature to dark purple or bluish-black fruits (drupes) that resemble Kalamata olives, but are not edible.

The beautiful heartwood is light reddish to yellowish brown with black streaks. Wood used for adze handles, used even green as firewood. It can grow to a tree but is often forced to sprout from the base when attacked by the black twig borer which bores into trees allowing ambrosia beetles and their "cultivated fungus" to enter under the bark to feed on the cambium, killing the tree. Along the **Manukā Nature Trail**, it is more common to see this species in fruit. It is quite common, especially along the first part of the trail.

9. *Pisonia sandwicensis* -- Aulu
Endemic/Nyctaginaceae/Four O'Clock Family

A large shrub or small tree with soft brittle wood found in dry to mesic forests, rarely in wet gulches, from about 850 to over 3,400 feet. It is often a dominant tree in its habitat. These beautiful, large-leaved trees can grow to about 60 feet tall. Large leaves glossy green and opposite. The flowers are small and funnel-shaped, 5-lobed, white or pinkish to whitish-brown and slightly fragrant. The fruit is cigar-shaped about 1 ½ inches long and very sticky when ripe which attracts and traps insects and birds.

The early Hawaiians used the adhesive gum from Aulu for repairing bowls. The sticky fruit used to trap birds. The captured victims provided feathers for the strikingly colorful cloaks (capes), helmets, lei, images and kāhili (traditional feather work). Birds such as 'ō'ō and mamo were seasonally plucked of their few moulting yellow feathers and set free to grow more for the next season. However, this was not the case with the 'i'iwi

and 'apapane which are covered with red-colored feathers and would not survive the plucking. They were captured, plucked

and eaten. Resembles Papala (*Charpentiera* spp.) but it does not have the slightly raised rim around the leaf. It is in the same family as Bougainvillea. In **Manukā,** the leaves have galls probably caused by mites, fungi or insects.

10. *Urera glabra* -- Opuhe
Endemic/Urticaceae/Nettle

Evergreen tree found from 500-5500 ft. in elevation in moist forests. Grows to 35 ft. with straight trunk 1 ft. in diameter, long stout branches and slightly milky or watery sap. Bark gray, smooth, very fibrous. Elliptical wavy toothed leaves, numerous tiny flowers along twigs partly back of leaves, male and female on different trees. Leaves alternate, with leafstalks of 1-2 inches. Blades oblong or narrowly elliptical, 6–14 inches long and 1–5 inches wide, long-pointed at tip, blunt at base, finely wavy toothed in upper part, thin or thick and slightly fleshy, usually palmately three-veined at base, with 12–15 parallel straight sunken veins on each side, pale below and often hairy along veins. Microscopic mineral growths (cystoliths) like crystals are present. Flower clusters (cymes) at base of leaves or back of leaves, about 2–3 inches in diameter, much forked regularly by two. Dioecious, very numerous, without corolla. Male flowers 8–20 almost stalkless in rounded balls, each about 1/8 inch in diameter, composed of pale reddish to whitish 4–5 lobed calyx and five stamens. Female flowers with 3–4-toothed calyx bordered by a cup and pistil with ovary and yellow stigma. Fruits rounded, about 1/8 inch in diameter, with enlarged fleshy orange yellow calyx enclosing one seed (achene), elliptical and rough with yellow stigma.

The wood is soft and lightweight. The fibrous bark was used by the Hawaiians for fish nets and at times for tapa cloth. This species is not apparent at the sign near the pit crater and is rare in **Manukā**. Photo by Kim and Forest Starr.

11. *Freycinetia arborea* -- 'Ie'ie
Indigenous/Pandanaceae/Climbing Screwpine

Woody climber found from low to medium elevation, forms dense tangles over forest floor and wrapped around trunks of o'hia and koa, climbing high into the canopy. It attaches to host tree by aerial roots and also grows as a sprawling tangle on the forest floor. Shiny green leaves have pointed ends, spiny on the lower side of midrib and along edges. Leaves 16–30 inches long, up to 1.5 in wide and spirally arranged around branch ends. Flowers and fruit form at ends of stems surrounded by red or yellow bracts.

The bracts and fruit were a favorite food of the 'ō'ū, an extinct Hawaiian honeycreeper that dispersed seeds for small seeded, fleshy plants in low elevation forests. Also a favored food of the 'alalā (*Hawaiian crow, actually a raven)* which is extinct in the wild but there are attempts to reintroduce it. 'Ie'ie considered sacred and dedicated to the forest god Ku. Aerial roots and pounded fibers used for house construction and outrigger canoes, fish traps and sandals. Fruit eaten as famine food.

12. *Tetraplasandra hawaiiensis* -- 'Ohe mauka
Endemic/ Araliaceae/ Ginsing Family

Small to medium evergreen tree with very few branches, growing from 20 to 60 feet tall. Bark is gray and smooth, becoming fissured with age. Leaves thick, hairless above, covered with hairs below, giving it a powdery look, feather-like with the edges turned under, crowded at ends of twigs. Leaflets 5-21, thick, leathery and stiff. Flowers in umbrella-like clusters at end of branch, small, yellow-green, or pink, spreading on slender stalks all about the same length. Fruits are many, small, rounded and green to blackish or deep purple when ripe. Also known as *Polyscias hawaiensis*.

13. *Psilotum nudum* -- Moa
Indigenous/Psilotaceae/Whisk Fern

Very primitive widely distributed erect fern relative to 2 ft. tall, branching Y-like with leaves reduced to tiny scales; angular stems and tiny yellow balls where spores form, scattered along terminal segments. It grows on lava, the ground and in tree crooks. The stems are green and function as leaves. Among the upper scales are borne three-lobed yellow cases filled with many minute spores. A slender underground stem functions as a root and contains a tiny fungus that helps to absorb food and water. Children played a game with the stems where each player made a hook with two branches and entwined them. Players pulled branches apart wishbone fashion. The winner whose hook did not break would crow like a rooster. Moa means chicken in Hawaiian. The species name means naked.

14. *Coprosma menziesii* -- Pilo
Endemic/Rubiaceae/Coffee Family

Viny shrub or small tree with light green, simple, opposite, smooth edged leaves, short stalked, small elliptical with paired scale-like pointed hairy stipules remaining on the slender twigs; small greenish or white flowers; male and female on different plants, with 4–9-lobed, tubular corolla, one to many borne mostly at leaf bases; small, fleshy round yellow, orange to bright orange, yellowish-orange or black fruits with two nutlets. Fruit forms along branch at leaf bases rather than clustered at end of stem as in Kopiko, another coffee relative.

This is a variable genus. Hawaiian and scientific name refer to the foul odor produced by bruised parts of some plants. There are 14 species of shrubs and small trees of this genus in Hawaii, one indigenous, the others endemic. At higher elevations in the Manukā Forest Reserve, *C. ernodeoides* (nene dung) is common creeping on lava. It has small, dark green, needle-like leaves and numerous glossy black berries.

15. *Cibotium glaucum* -- Hapu'u
Endemic/Dicksoniaceae/True Tree Fern

Found in damp to dry forests up to 6,000 feet in elevation, associated with o'hia trees. They grow to 20 feet and 2 feet in diameter. Fronds distinctly whitish underneath (the species name means "grayish"). Stalks hairy at base. Fronds are triply compound. Sori form along the margins of the leaflets. Fiddleheads are edible. They are often uprooted by feral pigs. The Hapu'u at the sign in Manukā died sometime in 2010. Today there are no living specimens found along the **Manukā Nature Trail**. They can be found in the upper reaches of the Manukā Forest Reserve. This genus has 4 endemics. Pulu which is made of the brown hairs that cover the young fiddlehead as it uncoils is used to stuff mattresses and pillows.

16. *Stenogyne rugosa* -- Ma'ohi'ohi
Endemic/Lamiaceae/Hawaiian Mint

Viny herb with square stems and opposite oval leaves that taper to a point. Small whitish to dark maroon flowers with upper lip larger than lower. Small berries bluish-black when ripe.

This mint is in the same family as thyme, catnip and rosemary. Of the twenty species originally described in Hawai'i, four are now extinct and five endangered. None are common. Consider yourself lucky if you come across this mint along the **Manukā Nature Trail**. Photo by Kim and Forest Starr.

17. *Melicope radiata* -- Alani
Endemic/Rutaceae/Citris Family

Shrub or small understory tree to 18 ft. tall found from upper dry forest to wetter areas in mountains and bogs. New leaves shiny and covered with fine, soft, short, grayish hairs. Opposite or whorled oval or oblong leaves with prominent central vein. Upper leaf glossy often with edges curled under with an anise-citris odor when crushed; upper surface pale green, lower surface slightly paler and duller usually with reddish veins, opposite, thin, leathery, brittle, elliptic to ovate or sometimes almost round, inconspicuous, connected by a weakly arched vein close to margin. Flowers small, yellow, 1-3 borne in axils; petals small, sharp pointed, narrow, hairless. Fruit unusual, four-parted, each lobe forming a corner of a square. Capsules green to red-tinged. Seeds glossy black when ripe, 1-2 per carpel. In the same family as citrus fruits and formerly in the genus *Pelea*. There are 47 members of this endemic genus in Hawai'i.

18. *Hedyotis terminalis* -- Monono
Endemic/Rubiaceae/Coffee Family

A variable, viny shrub or small tree found in moderately wet to humid forests with opposite leaves that look like kissing lips, (the best distinguishing characteristic of members of the coffee family) when first emerging. Small grappling hook trumpet-shaped flowers purple on outside, green inside. Fruit purple-black and about ¼ inch in diameter. New name is *Kadua affinus*.

This photo shows the Mono-no fruit. There are 22 species of this genus, 20 are endemic, the other 2 introduced. The genus name means sweet ear referring to the sweet smelling leaves. Woody parts used for rigging and trimming outrigger canoes. Formerly known as *Gouldia terminalis*. Fruit photo by Kim and Forest Starr. Another species found near the coast is *H. littoralis* a small succulent herb with white 4-petaled star shaped flowers. It is rare.

19. *Pisonia brunoniana* -- Papala kepau
Indigenous/Nyctaginaceae/Four O'clock Family

Large shrub or tree up to 18 ft. tall; branchlets somewhat quadrangular, smooth or nearly so. Leaves large, blunt, oval and papery, growing in clusters, without a raised rim, usually opposite or occasionally in threes or whorled, broadly elliptic to elliptic-ovate or obovate, up to at least 8 inches long and 4 inches wide, main lateral nerves 6-12 pairs, apex usually obtuse, abruptly narrowed at base to slender, petioles to 1 ½ inches long. Flowers moderately fragrant, in semi-open cymes, becoming larger and very open in fruit, borne in upper axils and terminally, forming broad, rounded, many-flowered panicles, elongating in fruit, petals whitish to greenish or bronze-colored. Fruit very sticky, flattened elongated with ridges.

Similar to *Pisonia sandwicensis* also having small insect caused galls on leaves and a sticky gum (kepau) forms on the exterior of the fruit smeared on tree limbs to catch birds for their feathers. Resembles Papala. Related to Bougainvillea.

20. *Pittosporum hosmeri* -- Ho'awa
Endemic/Pittosporaceae/Kona Cheesewood

Gangly evergreen shrub or small tree ranging in height from 10 to 25 feet. The bark is smooth and mottled light gray and brown. The upright branches are slender and stiff and generally smooth, but new growth and flower stems are densely covered with woolly, pale brown hairs. The narrow, shiny, alternate, pointed, oblong leaves are somewhat leathery and range in size from 4 to 10 inches long and cluster near branch tips. The leaves are so crowded they can appear opposite. The veins are fairly prominent on the upper leaf surface and the lower surface is covered with light brown or pale brown woolly hairs. The edges of the leaves are smooth and slightly rolled under. Male and female flowers grow on separate plants so plants of both sexes are required for seed to form. The flower clusters contain 9 to 12 flowers and form either directly on the branches of the plant or from the base of the leaf stem. The cream-colored flowers are tubular and 1/4 to 1/2 inch long and are fragrant at night. Fruit resembles a walnut and seed capsules split open to reveal a bright orange lining and sticky black seeds. There are 12 species: 10 endemic, 2 introduced in Hawaii. Considered poisonous yet the pounded outer layer of the fruit used to cure sores. Wood sometimes used to make gunwales for canoes.

21. *Caesalpinia bonduc* -- Kakalaioa
Indigenous?/Fabaceae/Yellow Nickers

Vine-like shrub with doubly compound leaves with small hooked thorns on stems and leaf petiole to 5 ft. in height (unsupported) and 18 ft. or more in extension; stems up to 2 inches in diameter or more. Plants

usually have a single stem arising from the ground but often branch low on the stem. The leaves are doubly pinnately compound with four to nine pair of pinnae, each with four to eight pair of oblong to elliptic to oval leaflets. Stalks of yellow flowers come from the side or end of the stem. Prickly, inflated fruit are flattened oval shaped, and reddish-brown to brown when dry. Within each pod are one to three (usually two) smooth, hard, seeds that are olive drab in the pods and remain so until exposure

to the sun bleaches them to a light gray-green color. The Hawaiian name means prickly. It is unknown if this species is indigenous or an early introduction. The thorns and prickles suggest the latter as plants that evolved on the Hawaiian Islands, before the introduction of browsers, lost their defense mechanisms.

22. *Rest Stop:* From the rest stop, you can see an Ohi'a tree with aerial roots hanging from a limb. These fibrous roots aid the tree in collecting moisture. Be sure to follow the trail leading off to the right from the rest area.

23. *Hawaiian Cultural Site:* Surprisingly, little archeological research has been conducted here considering it has been protected under the Park system and is relatively untouched.

24. *Agricultural Mounds:* These earth mounds, ranging from 12 to 36 inches high, played a significant role in ancient Hawaiian agriculture. Hawaiians adapted to their landscape and built these small earth mounds to provide water for crops and to protect crops from the sun.

25. *Psychotria hawaiiensis* -- Kopiko
Endemic/Rubiaceae/Coffee Family

Large shrub or small tree common in wet forest environments with Ohi'a and tree ferns. It has glossy, opposite, pointed stiff oval leaves with small pits (piko) in the corner between midrib and side veins on underside of leaf which contain bacteria (*Azotobacter*) able to fix nitrogen. Erect flower stalk with small, white, star-shaped flowers and 4 or 5 petals at ends of leaf stalk. Fruit fleshy, drooping, orange, globose, about ½ inch long.

This genus includes 11 species endemic to Hawaii. The hard, whitish wood was used to make anvils for beating bark into kapa cloth and for firewood. Look for the "kissing lips" arrangement of the newly emerging leaves. Kopiko is a common species along the **Manukā Nature Trail**.

26. *Wikstroemia sandwicensis* -- 'Akia
Endemic/Thymelaeaceae/ Variableleaf False 'ōhelo

Spindly shrub or small tree with spindle shaped, opposite leaves on slender twigs with smooth bark often reddish tinged. Flowers small, yellow or yellowish-green, clustered trumpets. Twigs difficult to separate from stems. Used to poison fish and criminals in old Hawaiian times. Size and shape of leaves vary.

There are about a dozen endemic members of this genus all difficult to tell apart and in need of further study.

22

27. *Zingiber zerumbet* -- ʻAwapuhi
Polynesian/Zingiberaceae/Shampoo Ginger

Low growing plant to 2 feet tall with 12 blade-like leaves mixed with stalks. The leaves are thin and more or less hairy on the underside. A flowering stem, a foot tall or so, rises from the rhizome separate from the leaves. The flowering head is oblong in shape and 2 or 3 inches long, consisting of overlapping bracts which are green and tinged pink to red. They hide small, inconspicuous yellowish flowers, one or two opening at a time.

Oval red fruit emits a slimy liquid when squeezed. Aromatic underground stems (rhizomes) resemble roots of culinary ginger (*Z. officinale*). Sap used by Hawaiians as a shampoo. Underground stems used to scent kapa. Medicinally used to treat headache, toothache, ringworm and skin diseases. May no longer grow near sign. Photo by Kim and Forest Starr.

28. *Alyxia oliviformis* -- Maile
Endemic/Apocynaceae/Dogbane Family

Twining vine or erect shrub which grows up and around other plants in wet to dry forests up to 6,000 ft. in elevation with small, shiny, smooth, pointed oval dark green opposite leaves that exude a milky sap. Flowers are small and yellowish and the ½ inch long; fruit resembles olives.

Plant form, leaf size and scent varies from plant to plant. All parts of the plant contain coumarin which gives it its pleasant fragrance. It is in the same family as Plumaria. Many songs, chants and hulas were inspired by this much-loved, sweet-scented plant and it was one of five plants dedicated to the hula goddess Laka.

29. *Styphelia tameiameiae* -- Pukiawe
Indigenous/Epacridaceae/Epacris Family

Small to large shrub or small tree found in low, dry forests and upper semi-arid subalpine scrub and exposed lava fields up to 10,000 ft. in elevation. It has many small, oval, hemlock needle-like leaves spiraling around stem. Green gray above, lighter beneath.

Flowers small and inconspicuous, white. Berries vary in color from white to pink to red or mottled. Fruit a favorite Nene food and strung into lei by Hawaiians. The leaves were used medicinally and the wood used to cremate criminals. It was believed the burning wood wards off their spirits. This family is closely related to the Heather Family (Ericaceae).

30. *Myrsine lessertiana* -- Kolea Lau Nui
Endemic/Myrsinaceae/Myrsine Family

Shrub or tree with rough gray bark and colorful young leaves unfurling from a conical bud with small woody knobs along the sides of older twigs. Thick leaves with prominently contrasting dark red colored mid veins. Small reddish flowers and shiny black cherry-like fruit form densely along bare areas on branches below leaf clusters.

The sap in the wood is red. Wood used in house and canoe construction and to make kapa beaters and dyes. There are 20 endemic species of *Myrsine* in Hawai'i.

31. *Antidesma pulvinatum* -- Hame
Endemic/Euphorbiaceae/Spurge Family

Trees up to 40 ft. tall with thinly furrowed gray bark. Leaves alternate, pointed and broadly oval. The leaf stems are short, stout,strongly curved to form a hook so the leaves lie in a plane along the twig. Flowers small, inconspicuous and form in leaf axils. Fruit in clusters, reddish to purple resembling M&Ms.

Leaves of this species of Hame can be green and bronze to shades of reds. The hard, red-brown wood used to make anvils for beating Olona fibers. The fruit used to make a red to purple dye to color kapa cloth. This is one of two endemic species in Hawaii. The other species is *A. platyphyllum.* Photo of the males flowers by David Eickhoff.

32. *Ageratina riparia* -- Hamakua pamakani
Introduced/Asteraceae/Sunflower Family

Sprawling herb with toothed, spindle-shaped leaves and flowers occurring in crowded clusters on erect stems lacking petals and appearing fuzzy and white.

Native of Mexico and the West Indies, first found in Hawai'i in 1926. Common weed.

33. *Hibiscus tiliaceus* -- Hau
Indigenous (maybe)/Malvaceae/Mallow Family

Large, spreading often prostrate tree that creates dense tangles at low elevation. Leaves are broadly round and heart-shaped, 3 to 12" in each dimension, slightly fuzzy under the leaf. Flowers yellow with 5 petals, deep red centers fading to burnt orange color later in the day.

Outrigger booms made from branches. Flowers have a laxative effect. Young leaf buds chewed for dry throat. A branch was set in the ground before battle. The side that was defeated would let their branch fall.

Species without signs:

TREES AND SHRUBS:

Charpentiera ovata -- Papala
Endemic/Amaranthaceae/Amaranth Family

Small tree to 35 feet with large, smooth, alternate oval leaves 6 to 12" long. They look similar and grow with Papala kepau (*Pisonia* spp. in family Nyctaginaceae) but feel for the raised margin on the papala leaf which are alternate, lance-like and leathery. Young leaves slightly to densely hairy. Numerous tiny flowers and seeds borne in long thread-like branched fruiting structures from the leaf axils.

Hawaiians would rub dry branches of this plant with kukui nut oil, ignite them and throw them to the sea as a form of fireworks.

Flueggea neowawraea -- Mehamehame
Endemic/ Phyllanthaceae/Leaf Flower Family

This tree grew as tall as 100 ft. and 7 feet in diameter and is virtually extinct following the accidental introduction of the black twig borer *Xylosandrus compactus* from Japan in 1931. On the Big Island, populations only exist on the Kona coast. Nearly all living individuals exist as basal shoots from older trees where the main trunk has died, or as out planted saplings. The wood is extremely durable and easily recognized due to its fluted pattern. Dead trunks can still be found. This tree does not grow near the **Manukā Nature Trail.** Photo by David Eickhoff.

Gouania vitifolia -- O'ahu Chewstick
Endemic/Endangered/Buckthorn Family

Climbing shrub or woody vine with tendrils found in dry, coastal mesic, and mixed mesic forests. It has small leaves that are papery with moderate to dense soft hairs covering both sides of the leaf. Leaves are elliptic to broadly oval, 1 to 3 inches long with toothed margins.

Found only in the Ka'u district of the Big Island and on O'ahu in the Wai'anae Mountains. In 2007 there were 64 plants left on Oahu and two populations numbering under 100 on the Big Island. It is threatened by alien plants and habitat destruction by feral pigs. Its common name comes from its use in oral hygiene. Finding this species along the **Manukā Nature Trail** will be sure to raise a stir with its finder. Photo by David Eickhoff.

Senna gaudichaudii -- Kolomona
Indigenous/Fabaceae/Scrambled Egg Tree

A shrub to 16 ft. tall with evenly pinnately compound leaves typical of Pea Family members. Flowers in racemes (an inflorescence in which the individual flowers are borne on slender stalks along a more or less elongated axis with the youngest flower at the top) with greenish-white to pale yellow flowers. Its pods drupe and are flat and are about 5 inches long. The reddish brown seeds are in narrow compartments in a single row.

This is the only indigenous member of this genus in Hawai'i but more work on this genus is needed. It is found around the Pacific Basin. Members of this genus used to treat constipation.

Piper methysticum -- Kava
Polynesian/ Piperaceae/Pepper Family

Small tree from 4 to 12 ft. tall with large, heart-shaped leaves about 5 to 8 inches long and green branches with pronounced swollen nodes where leaves attach. Leaf veins have 11 to 13 prominent, palmately arranged veins; meaning they all originate at the leaf base and curve, approaching one another at the tip. Male and female flowers borne on narrow spikes on separate plants. Color of the stem varies with variety.

Pulverized roots used to produce an intoxicant called 'awa. Hawaiians offered a niu (coconut) shell cup of 'awa to a visitor as a sign of hospitality. To offset the unpalatability of the drink, they would eat a small banana as a pupu. This word came to mean an hors d'oeuvre eaten with a pre-meal drink. Small quantities produce euphoria. Larger quantities affect vision and muscle coordination. Medicinally this plant was used for kidney disorders, thrush, insomnia and headaches.

Schinus terebinthifolius -- Christmasberry
Introduced/Anacardiaceae/Sumac Family

Low growing shrub or small tree found from sea level to 4,000 feet in elevation. Leaves alternate along opposite sides of twigs in 2, 3, 4 or more pair of ¾ to 3 inch long oval leaflets with an odd one at the tip. Crushed leaves have a strong, peppery fragrance. May cause allergic reactions in some people. Introduced from Brazil in 1941, this is one of the worst invasive plants in dry forests. It is allelopathic, meaning it produces chemicals that prohibit other species from growing under it. The berries are poisonous. In Manukā, an attempt has been made to eradicate this species. Instead of using toxic chemicals, the trees are girdled, meaning a cut is made through the bark all around the tree which kills the tree since it disrupts the cambium layer where nutrients and water are transported.

Psidium cattleianum -- Strawberry Guava
Introduced/Myrtaceae/Myrtle Family

Small bush or tree to 20-25 ft., although often smaller. The bark is splotchy with grayer patches where the bark is peeling off. The fruit is red or rarely yellow and small, to 1.5" around. The pulp is translucent and very juicy.

For a beautiful tree with such tasty fruit, this is yet another invasive plant in Hawai'i. It forms dense thickets and eventually pure forests, under which few other plants grow. It is eaten by pigs which move into infested areas during the fruiting season. The seeds pass through digestive tracts unharmed and are often deposited in soil disturbed by pigs. The wood is used for walking sticks. In same family as eucalyptus, cloves, allspice and ohi'a.

Psidium guajava -- Common Guava
Introduced/Myrtaceae/Myrtle Family

A small tree to 33 ft. tall, with spreading branches, smooth, thin, copper-colored bark that flakes off, with a greenish layer beneath; trunk appears bone-like and may reach a diameter of 10 in. Young twigs quadrangular and downy. The leaves, aromatic when crushed, have an odor reminiscent of apple, and are evergreen, opposite, short stalked, oval or oblong-elliptic, somewhat irregular in outline; leathery, with conspicuous parallel veins, more or less downy on the underside. Faintly fragrant, the white flowers, appear singly or in small clusters in leaf axils, with 4 or 5 white petals that quickly fall off, leaving a prominent tuft of ~250 white stamens tipped with pale-yellow anthers. The fruit is similar to the Strawberry Guava but larger with light-yellow skin, frequently blushed pink. The central pulp is juicy with very hard, yellowish seeds, rarely with soft, chewable seeds. Some guavas are seedless or nearly so. When immature and until a very short time before ripening, the fruit is green, hard, gummy within and astringent. Like Strawberry Guava, this species is invasive.

Coffea arabica -- Coffee
Introduced/Rubiaceae/Coffee Family

Naturalized plants grow to 36 ft. tall with an open branching system; the leaves are opposite, simple, elliptic-ovate to oblong, broad, and glossy dark green. The flowers are white and grow in clusters from the leaf axils. The fruit is a drupe (though commonly called a "berry"), maturing bright red to purple and typically containing two seeds (the coffee "bean"). The Coffee Family is also known as the Madder or Bedstraw Family.

Annona cherimola -- Cherimoya
Introduced/Annonaceae/Custard Apple Family

Small tree to 25 ft. tall. The leaves are alternate, simple, oblong to lance-shaped. The flowers are produced in small clusters, each flower has six petals that are yellow-brown and often spotted purple at the base. Fruit same color as leaves, heart shaped and blend in with the foliage. They taste like a blend of pineapple, strawberry and mango. Delicious!

The cherimoya is considered one of the best-tasting fruits in the world. Seeds are hard and have medicinal and toxic qualities. Native to the Andean-highland valleys of Bolivia, Chile, Colombia, Ecuador and Peru. There are several Cherimoya trees along the **Manukā Nature Trail** that I have only found in fruit once. Photo by Kim and Forest Starr.

Homalanthus populifolius -- Bleeding Heart
Introduced/Euphorbiaceae/Spurge Family

A small tree or shrub up to 25 ft. tall. The trunk is cylindrical with grayish brown bark, fairly smooth but with some bumps and irregularities. Branchlets appear thick, reddish or green. The leaves are triangular, untoothed and alternate, turning red with age, giving the plant its common name. Flowers are yellow-green to red, on racemes (meaning a simple inflorescence in which the flowers are borne on short stalks of about equal length at equal distances along an elongated axis). The fruit is a 2-lobed capsule with an oily aril (the fleshy, usually brightly colored cover of a seed).

This species is spreading along the **Manukā Nature Trail** and can also be seen in the pit crater. It is native to the Australian rainforest where it often appears in areas of rainforest disturbance. Bleeding Heart is highly regarded by rainforest regenerators due its fast growth and used as a pioneering species in rainforest regeneration elsewhere on the planet. It is an invasive species in Hawaii. Also known as Queensland Poplar.

Pluchea symphytifolia -- Sourbrush
Introduced/Asteraceae/Sunflower Family

A shrub common in disturbed areas to 15 ft. tall. Its unpleasant odor is the best way to distinguish this plant. It has woolly, oblong, green-gray leaves that are up to 8 inches long and 3 inches wide. Flowers are in large unattractive flat-topped clusters. Native to Mexico and the West Indies, it showed up in Hawai'i in 1931 and is now widespread.

Ochna serrulata -- Mickey Mouse Plant
Introduced/Ochnaceae/Ochna Family

A shrub to 15 ft. tall. The serrated leaves have little to no stem and are closely attached to the twig. Flowers are yellow with 5 petals. The fruit consists of several oval, glossy green turning black seeds borne on a bright red flower-like receptacle. Sometimes the fruit resembles the head and large round ears of Mickey Mouse. The seeds are oily and protein rich and are food for introduced birds which spread them, making this a serious pest in dry to mesic forests. Native to east tropical Africa, it became naturalized along the trail from cultivated plants in the Manuka Plantation.

Herbs:

Dianella sandwicensis -- 'Uki'Uki
Indigenous/Liliaceae/Lily Family

Common in mesic forests but also found in dry shrub land and wet forests. It has smooth, glossy strap leaves that arise from clumps of stems. It has a prominent central vein running the length of the leaf. This feature distinguishes it from the common sedge with the same name ('Uki). It produces many, small, six petalled flowers about 1/2 inch in diameter and pale blue to purplish 1/2 inch long berries.

The fruits are used to prepare a blue or blue-purple dye or strung with greenery to make leis. Also, the leaves were used as thatch. May be assigned to family *Phormiaceae*. I have found this species in only one place along the **Manukā Nature Trail**.

Castilleja arvensis -- Field Paintbrush
Introduced/Scrophulariaceae/Snapdragon Family

It is the only paintbrush in Hawai'i with red bracts. The greenish flowers are in hairy, elongated flower spikes with red-tipped, petal-like bracts. The leaves are green, stalkless, alternate, 3-veined, and linear-elliptic, lance-like, or much longer than wide and with the widest portion near the tip The stems are erect, densely hairy, and usually unbranched. The plants are partial root parasites of nearby plants.

This naturalized annual species which grows to 32 inches tall, is native to Mexico, Central and South America. Naturalized in Hawai'i in disturbed areas and on lava flows.

Peperomia tetraphylla -- Four-leaved Peperomia
Indigenous/Piperaceae/Pepper Family

 Small decumbent or erect herb to 8 inches long, rooting at the nodes. Stems green to reddish-purple, usually several from a common base. Leaves in whorls of 3 or 4, elliptic to broadly egg-shaped, base wedge-shaped to rounded, margins entire (not toothed) somewhat smooth and glossy above. Tiny flowers form on a unique spike at the branchlet end.

It isalso native to Australia, Asia, Africa, New Zealand and other islands in the Pacific Ocean and often seen as an epiphyte or growing on rocks in rainforests. It is also known as the Acorn Peperomia.

Rubus rosifolius -- Akala
Introduced/Rosaceae/Thimbleberry

 This weedy raspberry grows in moist, open, disturbed sites. Leaves are alternate and pinnately compound with 3, or 7 green, ovate to lance-shaped leaflets with doubly serrate (teeth on teeth) margins. Stems are hairy, sparsely covered with sharp prickles and erect, arching, or trailing. The flowers have 5 white, egg-shaped petals and 5 hairy, green, lance-shaped sepals with long, pointed, tapering tips. The flowers are followed by green, ripening to ruby red, edible raspberries.

This species is a serious pest in forests and was introduced in the 1880's. Also known as West Indian Raspberry, it is native to Asia and Australia. There are 7 species of this genus in Hawaii, 2 are endemic including *R. hawaiensis* ('Akala is related to *R. spectabilus*: salmonberry) and *R. macraei*, both with dark pink to dusky rose (or rarely white for *R. hawaiensis)* petals.

Solanum americanum -- Popolo
Naturalized/Solanaceae/ Glossy Nightshade

Annual or short lived perennial to 3 ft. tall. Leaves simple and alternate. The flowers are small and white or occasionally light purple, with a yellowish green, star-shaped area. Berries glossy black.

Popolo was used medicinally by Hawaiians for diseases of the digestive tract and sore throat. Also the young shoots used as a pot herb in New Guinea and other Pacific islands. The earliest collection of this species was in 1835 though it is possible this species arrived here before Captain Cook did. This is a highly variable species.

ALL OTHERS: Vines, Ferns, a Fungus, and a Grass

Ipomoea indica -- Blue Morning Glory
Indigenous/Convolvulaceae/Bindweed Family

A tough, trailing, perennial vine with many branching stems. It can grow to 25 feet, up and over shrubs and small trees or form a dense carpet. Leaves heart-shaped. Flowers delicate blue, purple or white. Fruit is a small, brown, spherical to flattened capsule which floats easily on water with one to four, dark brown, rounded and smooth seeds.

Pounded stems and roots used as medicine for aches, pains and constipation. All parts of the plant can have a dangerous cathartic effect. Used as a poultice for wounds, sores and broken bones. The bark of the roots and plant mixed with salt and applied to wounds with a ki leaf between the wound and the poultice. In same genus as the indigenous Beach Morning Glory (*I. pes-caprae*) pohuehue.

Cocculus tribolus -- Huehue
Indigenous/Menispermaceae/Moonseed Family

Slender vine common in dry and mesic forests. It has alternate, oval or pointed leaves with three main veins running from base to tip. It has yellowish-white bluntly-tipped star-shaped flowers in small clusters at base of leaves. Fruit is a dark berry on the female plant. It may be confused with the introduced *Passiflora suberosa* except for the three veins. Huehue is used to anchor thatch to structures and as twine.

Nephrolepis exaltata -- Kupukupu
Endemic/Nephrolepidaceae/Sword Fern

Common in upper dry to wet forests. Long and strap-like fronds, not tapering except at the tip like a sword. Blade composed of two rows of pinnately compound, oblong leaflets, each tapering to a sharp or rounded point. Small, round, sori occur in a row on each side of the midrib of each leaflet.

This is the most common fern along the **Manukā Nature Trail**. It is native to tropical regions throughout the world and is common in humid forests and swamps in northern South America, Mexico, Central America, Florida, the West Indies, Polynesia and Africa. It is also known as the Wild Boston fern but differs from the Swordfern (*Polystichum munitum*) common in the Pacific Northwest.

Pleopeltis thunbergiana -- Pakahakaha
Indigenous/Polypodiaceae/Common Fern Family

This fern has leathery fronds that are yellowish-green to dark green and white on the underside. They can reach 15 inches in length. Spores form in round to oval, cinnamon brown pockets. This species is wide-spread and can grow on the ground or as an epiphyte (growing on other species) and tends to curl up in dry weather.

Cyrtomium falcatum -- Ka'ape'ape
Naturalized/Aspidiaceae/Holly Fern

The fronds are thick, glossy and leathery. Pinnae (the primary division of the blade) 5-14. Stem to 2 ft. tall with brown scales at the base. The undersides are covered with sori, the spore bearing part of a fern. A common fern in disturbed areas native to eastern Asia. There is a rare native species: *C. caryotideum* which does not have such glossy blades and it has less pinna pairs. Other ferns you may encounter along the **Manukā Nature Trail** include the Maile-scented Fern (*Phymatosorus grossus*) and the Maidenhair Spleenwort (*Asplenium trichomanes).* The False Staghorn Fern (*Dicranopteris linearis*) is occasional higher up in the **Manukā Forest Reserve.**

Pycnoporus sanguineus -- Scarlet Wood Fungus
Indigenous/Polyporaceae

One of the more common shelf polypores (meaning it has pores instead of gills or teeth on the lower cap) in Hawaii. The tough, bright red shelves with or without stems, are found on stumps, logs and branches.

It is a plant pathogen common in tropical and subtropical regions of the world. Fruiting bodies may grow individually or clustered, sometimes overlapping. Some of the most distinguishing characteristics of the caps other than the color are their texture. In general, caps appear to be smooth, leathery, or corky in appearance. A dye can be made from the fruiting bodies. There are other fungi that occur along the **Manukā Nature Trail**. Refer to the field guide ***Mushrooms of Hawai'i*** for identification. Also be on the lookout for some of our other non-flowering species including lichens, mosses, algae and liverworts.

Monstera deliciosa -- Swiss Cheese Plant
Introduced/Araceae/Arum Family

Tree climbing vine able to grow up to 65 feet tall with large, leathery, glossy, roughly heart-shaped leaves that are thick and waxy, growing up to three feet long and wide with split sections running horizontally. Young plants have leaves that are smaller and entire with no lobes or holes, but soon produce lobed and holed leaves. It has a thick green stem that can reach up to three inches thick and produces numerous aerial roots that attach to its support. The plants have calla lily-like flowers that become fruit shaped like an ear of corn.

This plant is mildly invasive in Hawai'i. The species name *deliciosa* refers to the edible fruit. All parts of the plant except the ripe fruit are poisonous. Fruit must be ripe to safely eat due to oxalate crystals common in members of the Arum Family. This species is found around the **Manukā Plantation** but also at the very end of the **Manukā Nature Trail**. Also known as Split Leaf Philodendron.

Oplismenus hirtellus -- Honohono kukui
Invasive/ Poaceae/ Basketgrass, Bamboo Grass

A grass to 3 ft. tall with a distinctive erect, columnar habit and curly leaves. It is orange-brown in color, fading to straw-color. The seed is surrounded by white, short hairs, giving the seed head a fluffy appearance. Mostly restricted to disturbed sites but it has taken over trail side and has shown itself capable of invading adjacent forests. It may create a fire hazard. Another invasive grass along the trail is Molasses Grass (*Melinis minutiflora*) which is hairy and sticky near the base and has an obvious molasses-like odor.

Jasminum polyanthum -- White Jasmine
Naturalized/Oleaceae/Olive Family

An evergreen twining climber with thin-leathery leaves pinnately compound and opposite with 5 to 7 leaflets which are dark green on the upper surface and lighter green on the lower surface. It produces an abundance of reddish-pink flower buds followed by fragrant, five-petalled, star-like, white with red on the inside flowers. The terminal leaflet is noticeably larger than the other leaflets.

The plant is very vigorous and can grow up to 20 ft. in height when supported. The tough, wiry stems travel long distances along the ground, often rooting at the leaf nodes and sucker from the roots. The stems climb vigorously into the tree canopy, blanketing other vegetation. White Jasmine is native to China. It was first noticed along the **Manukā Nature Trail** in 2004.

Senecio mikanoides -- German Ivy
Introduced/Asteraceae/Sunflower Family

A vine that climbs up trees and will reach heights of over 16 ft. Given time, it smothers trees. It has 2 to 4 -inch, multi-lobed leaves that somewhat resemble those of the unrelated English ivy. Its flowers are yellow. It is an invasive species in Hawaii and covers shrubs and trees, inhibiting growth and will also cover ground intensively over a wide area as it is doing along the Manukā Trail. It prevents seeds of other species from germinating or growing. Native to South Africa. Also known as *Delairea odorata.*

Passiflora mollissima -- Banana Poka
Introduced/Passifloriaceae/Passion-flower Family

This common vine has deeply lobed, 3-fingered leaves. The flowers of this pesky plant are beautiful. Ten large, pink petals emerge at right angles to a tube with a bulbous base. The fruit is long, yellow and banana like.

This species is a serious pest in Hawai'i. It was allegedly introduced to hide an outhouse in the early 1900's. It takes over native trees and shrubs and is widely distributed by feral pigs and other animals. While this is the most common Passiflora (Liliko'i) along the **Manukā Nature Trail**, *P. edulis* (the more well known passion fruit) and *Passiflora ligularis* (Sweet Granadilla) are here too.

Cecropia obtusifolia -- Trumpet Tree
Planted and naturalized/Cecropiaceae/Cecropia

This species is included here because it is evidence of the changes the vegetation along the **Manukā Nature Trail** is going through. Many species introduced by people have found it easy to take over and reproduce in ways that over run the native species, so special to the Hawaiian Islands. These native species--many growing along the Trail--are found nowhere else on the planet.

The Trumpet Tree first collected on Hawai'i in 1926, is native from southern Mexico to Ecuador and Columbia. It is now naturalized in pastures and low elevation mesic to wet forests on Kaua'i, O'ahu and the Big Island. It was planted in the **Manukā Plantation** and can now be found not far along on the **Manukā Nature Trail.**

I hope you enjoyed the information in this guide. More and more non-native species are finding their way into the Manukā NAR. If you find species that should be added to this book, please let me know at judyinhaines@aptalaska. net. Mahalo!

See you on the Trail. *A hui hou!*

Native Birds to look for at Manukā, especially around the Pit Crater

Photos: Manukā Pit Crater, ʻElepaio, ʻApapane and ʻAmakihi

REFERENCES

Friday, J.B., and D.A. Herbert. 2006. Metrosideros polymorpha ('ōhi'a), ver. 3.2. In: Elevitch, C.R. (ed.). Species Profiles for Pacific Island Agroforestry. Permanent Agriculture Resources (PAR), Hōlualoa, Hawai'i.

Hall, John B. 2004. *A Hiker's Guide to Trailside Plants in Hawai'i.* Honolulu:Mutual Publishing.

Hargreaves, Dorothy and Bob. 1964. *Tropical Trees of Hawaii.* Portland, OR: Hargreaves Industrial

Hemmes, Don E., and Dennis Desjatdin. 2002. *Mushrooms of Hawai'i.* Berkeley:Ten Speed Press

Kimura, Bert Y. and Kennet N. Nagata. 1980. *Hawaii's Vanishing Flora.* The Oriental Publishing Company.

Krause, Beatrice H. 1993. *Plants in Hawaiian Medicine.* Ill.Thelma Grieg. Honolulu:University of Hawai'i Press.

-----------. *2001. Plants in Hawaiian Culture.* Ill. Martha Noyes. Honolulu:The Bess Press

Merlin, Mark. 1999. *Hawaiian Forest Plants: an illustrated Field Guide.* Pacific Guide Books.

Palmer, Daniel D. 2003. *Hawai'i's Ferns and Fern Allies.* Honolulu:University of Hawai'i Press

Pratt, Douglas H. 1999. *A Pocket Guide to Hawai'i's Trees and Shrubs.* Honolulu:Mutual Publishing.

Scott, Susan. 1991. *Plants and Animals of Hawaii.* Bess Press.

Staples, George W. and Robert H. Cowie. 2001. *Hawai'i's Invasive Species.* Mutual Publishing.

Stone, Charles P. and Linda W. Pratt. 1994. *Hawai'i's Plants and Animals; Biological Sketches of Hawaii Volcanoes National Park.* Hawaii Natural History Association, US Park Servvice and University of Hawaii.

Walther, Michael. 2004. A *Guide to Hawai'i's Coastal Plants.* Honolulu:Mutual Publishing

Wagner, W.L., D.R. Herbst and S.H. Sohmer. 1999. *Manual of the Flowering Plants of Hawai'i.* Bishop Museum Special Publ. 83. Honolulu: Univ. Hawai'i and Bishop Museum. 2 volumes.

Wood, Paul. 2007. *Tropical Trees of Hawaii.* Island Heritage Publishing

Index

Field Notes

Field Notes

Field Notes